One-Minute Prayers™

FOR *Singles*

Text by
HOPE LYDA

HARVEST HOUSE PUBLISHERS

EUGENE, OREGON

ONE-MINUTE PRAYERS is a series trademark of The Hawkins Children's LLC. Harvest House Publishers, Inc., is the exclusive licensee of the trademark ONE-MINUTE PRAYERS.

Cover by Garborg Design Works, Minneapolis, Minnesota

Cover photo © José Carlos Pires Pereira/iStockphoto.com

ONE-MINUTE PRAYERS™ FOR SINGLES
Copyright © 2006 by Harvest House Publishers
Eugene, Oregon 97402
www.harvesthousepublishers.com

ISBN-13: 978-0-7369-1717-9
ISBN-10: 0-7369-1717-9
Product # 6917179

Printed in the United States of America

06 07 08 09 10 11 12 13 14 / BP-MS / 10 9 8 7 6 5 4 3 2 1

Contents

On My Way

It is God who arms me with strength and makes my way perfect.

PSALM 18:32

I am officially on my way to becoming an adult. Maybe I am a bit behind schedule, but now—now I feel that I am taking care of my responsibilities. I'm managing my home, my job, and my plans. I've started thinking about the future more so I can be prepared. It feels good to be independent of others and have confidence in my decisions.

Through Your strength, I can stand on the foundation of my life and look forward to all You have for me.

Fulfillment

Stepping Toward Fulfillment

"Love your neighbor as yourself." Love does no harm to its neighbor. Therefore love is the fulfillment of the law.

ROMANS 13:9-10

Lord, You have shown me that the key to life, to connection, to relationship, and to purpose is to love. May I have the strength to draw inspiration and motivation from Your love so that I may share it with others—that I might experience deep fulfillment.

I am not sure I know how to define "fulfillment." But sometimes I get a glimpse of what it looks like in the smile of others; I get a feel for it when I sense Your hand on my life. Teach me to truly understand what it means to be filled by love's grace. And when I have understanding, teach me to move deeper into the offerings of a fulfilled life.

Refresh Me

I will refresh the weary and satisfy the faint.

JEREMIAH 31:25

The ads on television for soft drinks and sports beverages always leave me thirsty. Everyone looks so refreshed and satisfied. God, I want that kind of refreshment for my spirit. There are days the grit of life fills the crevices of my spirit. The responsibilities I face weigh on me, and the work seems to use up each day's strength.

Guide me toward the people, the activities, the healthy thinking that will refresh me and fulfill my desire to have energy and passion for life. I want to be my best. Lord, lift me with Your Word and Your hope.

My First Glance

Satisfy us in the morning with your unfailing love,
that we may sing for joy and be glad all our days.

PSALM 90:14

Lately I have been wishing I was sharing my life with someone. I have my friends and family members, and my life is rich in many ways. But there are times when I would love to call a special person and tell him or her about my day.

This morning I was awakened by the sun shining through my bedroom blinds. At first I hid from the harsh, natural alarm clock, and then I let myself sit back and enjoy the warmth of a new day's greeting. Lord, You are so faithful. You give me everything I need for each moment, each day, each stretch of my path. You are the first one I come to with my troubles, my joys, and my day. Thank You.

Taking Vows

*Then will I ever sing praise to your name and
fulfill my vows day after day.*

PSALM 61:8

God, the day I made my commitment to follow
You and seek Your heart, I entered into a covenant that
would impact my life forever. Today I felt as though I
didn't fulfill my part of the covenant. I let go when I
should have held on tighter.

But after watching my married friends deal with
their own ups and downs and joys and trials, I realize
that the act of taking a vow ushers us into a living,
breathing, changing relationship. This is a relationship
of grace.

I sing Your praises today, Lord, because Your covenant remains unbroken. And I sing praises because I
long to fulfill my vows of faith in Your presence.

Balance

Standing on Now

The end of a matter is better than its beginning,
and patience is better than pride.

ECCLESIASTES 7:8

People like to say that everything turns out in the end. I say it too, God. But sometimes I don't believe it. When I wonder what my life might have looked like if I had done this or decided that, the "what ifs" never result in real answers. I want balance in my life. I don't want to question the past or predict the future. With Your strength I can stand in the perfect center—the immediate moment—and find balance.

Lord, grant me patience. When my desire to do it all or have it all takes on the shape of pride, relieve me from this burden. I pray to trust Your provision because the end, the middle, and even my now is in Your hands.

Holistic Holiness

*And we pray this in order that you may live a life
worthy of the Lord and may please him in every
way: bearing fruit in every good work, growing
in the knowledge of God, being strengthened with
all power according to his glorious might so that
you may have great endurance and patience,
and joyfully giving thanks to the Father, who has
qualified you to share in the inheritance of the
saints in the kingdom of light.*

COLOSSIANS 1:10-12

God of love and light, You are my beacon and my
guide. Only You can make me complete. Only Your
knowledge leads to my future. When I am scattered
or uncertain, Your wisdom brings unity and certainty
to my life.

May the work of my hands and mind always be
pleasing to You. When I walk in Your ways, my step is
steady and in line with my purpose. Let me bear fruit
in everything I do. As every part of me sings out to
praise You for Your mercy and joy, may I celebrate the
wholeness that only You can give.

Solo Act

*Plans fail for lack of counsel, but with many
advisers they succeed.*

PROVERBS 15:22

God, did You see me in the limelight? I took a bow;
I took requests; I even took responsibility for getting
there. How silly I was. Why didn't I see how false this
success was? That it wasn't mine and that it was not
blessed by You.

I didn't want anyone else's opinion about what I
was doing or how I was doing it. I felt that as long as I
was successful in the world's eyes, I must be on track.
You have shown me, through the goodness and guidance of others who trust in You, that there is a different
way. It turns out that I was standing on the wrong stage
all along. I'm not meant to be a solo act. I was born to
star in the life You are directing for me.

I Went That-a-Way

Come near to God and he will come near to you.

JAMES 4:8

∽

I ran for miles and miles while searching for Your truth and Your direction for my situation. Maybe I felt that if I pushed the limits, You would have to come and save me. But when I got lost in the wilderness of my choices and my circumstances, I saw how far away I was from my original faith.

You are full of surprises, Lord. You remind me of the simple truth I had forgotten. All I need to do is draw near to Your heart, and You are there. You are not in a different country, a different job, a different stage of life—You are right here.

Priorities

Lead On

*Direct me in the path of your commands, for there
I find delight.*

PSALM 119:35

God, when I look back over my life, I see how
often and how easily I change my priorities. I turn to
face whatever catches my attention—a love interest, a
career goal, a new style, a way of life. I can lose sight of
the delights intended for my vision, for my journey.

Lead me, Lord. Direct my days and my decisions
so that my priorities line up with Your will. Allow me
to discern Your commands that sound out against
the soundtrack of my past priorities. I want to know
delights that come from Your hand.

What I Give Up

*To do what is right and just is more acceptable to
the LORD than sacrifice.*

PROVERBS 21:3

Lord, forgive me when I am in a woe-is-me mood.
Usually I am excited about life and the wonders You
offer each day. But sometimes all I can think about is
what I don't have or what I have given up. If I had
changed my priorities a few years ago, I might be in a
different state of being, or in a relationship, or pursuing
a different path. Yet that wouldn't have been the life
You called me to for now.

When I start counting all the things I give up to do
the right things and to live a godly life, remind me how
these are the thoughts of a selfish child, not of a person
growing in faith. I want to be mature in my spiritual
walk. I hope that on most days You will find my actions,
heart, and words acceptable and pleasing.

Humble Pie

He guides the humble in what is right and
teaches them his way. All the ways of the
LORD are loving and faithful for those who keep
the demands of his covenant.

PSALM 25:9-10

I don't often feast on humble pie, but when I do, I feel Your presence. In my most vulnerable moments I know who leads me, cares for me, and teaches me life lessons. God, when I am faced with mistakes or consequences, allow me to accept humility graciously. Forgive me for the times when I allowed embarrassment to void that lesson and that opportunity to be a model of gentleness.

Lord, my weakness is Your strength. May my priority to do well never rise above my priority to show Your mightiness—even in the midst of my failings.

Making It Count

But just as you excel in everything—in faith, in speech, in knowledge, in complete earnestness and in your love for us—see that you also excel in this grace of giving.

2 CORINTHIANS 8:7

I look around at all the blessings in my life. They are plentiful and abundant! Lord, I am thankful for the work You give to me and for the abilities I have. Help me discover the gifts and abilities You want me to develop and use to Your glory.

God, may I view my blessings—opportunities, material wealth, strengths—as my means to give. I am opening my eyes to all You have given to me. Now let me open my hands and my heart to give to others.

Peace

Cleared for Takeoff

I run in the path of your commands, for you have set my heart free.

PSALM 119:32

When I wait for the airplane to leave the runway I get anxious. What are they doing? What are they checking? Is the plane okay? Will I ever get to where I want to go? The peace comes after we are cleared for takeoff, and I rest easy when I am free to reach my destination.

Lord, while I wait for things to happen in my life, I get anxious. What are You doing? What will happen? Should I be checking that path instead of this one? My worries well up inside. The doubts begin. But then You clear the path with Your commands and Your will. The ride could still be bumpy, but the peace is within me. And no matter the destination, my heart is set free.

Protector

And the peace of God, which transcends all
understanding, will guard your hearts and your
minds in Christ Jesus.

PHILIPPIANS 4:7

I am fragile, Lord. When I spend time alone and begin to think through everything in my life, my guard comes down. In Your presence I reveal my fears and my hopes. You receive them and shape them into my future, and I feel comfort.

Even if I don't understand all there is to know about Your ways, I do understand the peace that comes over me when I give myself to You. It is not easy for me to trust people in my life. And when I do, I do so carefully and with reservation. But, Lord, when I sit before You, I know You are guarding my heart and mind. You are my Protector, and I can be me.

Like the Wind

*He replied, "You of little faith, why are you so
afraid?" Then he got up and rebuked the winds
and the waves, and it was completely calm. The
men were amazed and asked, "What kind of man
is this? Even the winds and the waves obey him!"*

MATTHEW 8:26-27

Lord, this certain situation I have been mulling over
for a while is getting to me. While talking to friends,
it was still in the back of my mind. It sits there and
takes up space. Soon it is all I can think about. Lord,
You calmed the seas with one command. You cleared
the disciples' fears and worries with the mention of
peace.

God, I want to be like the winds and waves that
obey Your word. I want to release the tossing and
turning of my concerns over to Your power. Give me
the peace of a sea that knows the voice of its Creator.

Easy

LORD, you establish peace for us; all that we have
accomplished you have done for us.

ISAIAH 26:12

You make my way easy, Lord. I praise You for all
that You have done for me and for those I love. Every
step of accomplishment in my life is taken on Your
strength and with Your guidance. When I am not in
line with what You want for my life, You are there to
see me through when I am willing to give up control.

God, You are mighty and gracious. I know that my
part of this relationship is easy when compared to all
that You do. You create life, and then You give it to me.
It is now my choice to give it back to You. Establish
peace in my life and in my heart.

Motivation

Reasons

*You need to persevere so that when you have
done the will of God, you will receive what he has
promised.*

HEBREWS 10:36

As a child I asked lots of questions. As Your child,
those questions still seem to rise up in my mind. You'd
think I would be past the question "Why?" now that I
can research topics, go online, and talk to people who
are wise. But my biggest whys relate to life's biggest
questions.

When I ask "Why am I here?" or "Why are You
asking me to do this?" I know that I have my answer—
when I do Your will, I am working toward Your promises. Right now...that is reason enough.

Permanent Press

*Not that I have already obtained all this, or have
already been made perfect, but I press on to take
hold of that for which Christ Jesus took hold of me.*

PHILIPPIANS 3:12

I love having a mission, Lord. Your love motivates
me to press on and take hold of all this life offers. I want
to see every opportunity You place before me. Give me
a heart large enough to take in every ounce of compassion and joy and pain intended for my journey.

Give me the strength to quit being motivated by
a drive to be perfect. Lord, my perfection is through
You. You have taken hold of me. Don't let go. You are
always the reason I press on.

Hunger

Blessed are those who hunger and thirst for
righteousness, for they will be filled.

MATTHEW 5:6

I have friends who are hungry only for love...or
for something that resembles it. They never get their
fill. They chase after it like it will save them. I admit
there have been times I thought this to be true. But
when I met You, I understood where my hunger came
from. It was so much deeper than a need for food, for
people, for status.

The satisfaction I receive from Your love cannot be
taken away. The gratitude I feel knowing You created
me just as I am is not an illusion. The wonder I feel
when I seek You and Your righteousness fills me and
will never subside.

Driven by Dollars

*Keep your lives free from the love of money and be
content with what you have, because God has said,
"Never will I leave you; never will I forsake you."*

HEBREWS 13:5

I want so much. And my motivation is not always
a good one. The pressure from our culture to gather,
store, and acquire more can get to me. I find myself
wanting more and more. Release me from the hold of
stuff and the desire for stuff. A lot of good can be done
with money, but it is the love of it that destroys people,
nations, relationships, and the spirit.

When I find my heart lusting for the material
world, remind me of Your love. No money can replace
Your presence and promises in my life. And if I am
tempted to give myself over to self-serving behavior,
remind me whom I truly serve.

Freedom

Go Walkabout

I will walk about in freedom,
for I have sought out your precepts.

PSALM 119:45

To the Aborigines, a walkabout is a ritual. It is the chance to break from the daily grind, seek solace, and then shake up the routine. Lord, You call us all to go walkabout. When we are mired in the rut of our life's busyness and under the weight of perceived pressures, You beckon our spirits to take a break.

Freedom is found in the gift of Your Spirit. If I only preoccupy myself and never invite silence or solace into my day, I miss out on this freedom. I pray I never let the sounds of my busy life crowd out Your voice calling me to embark on a journey.

Save My Place

*Now the Lord is the Spirit, and where the Spirit of
the Lord is, there is freedom.*

2 CORINTHIANS 3:17

Where You are, I want to be. Where You lead, I want
to follow. Where You sit, I want to rest beside You. I
think of Your Spirit as a river that flows through all
Your children. You breathe life into us and lead us to
freedom.

I sought the peace of Your grace long before I knew
You. When I tasted of Your everlasting mercy, I knew
You would always be with me. And I knew I would be
in Your care forevermore.

Emotional Poverty

*One man gives freely, yet gains even more;
another withholds unduly, but comes to poverty.*

PROVERBS 11:24

Lord, help me emulate those people in my life who give freely. I always know when I am in their presence because I feel free to be myself. Show me how I keep people from this freedom. When I speak words of gossip or undermine a person's worth, convict my spirit so that I might make it right.

There are many ways You give to me. Each time I am jealous or disapproving in a judgmental way, I am withholding Your love. I pray that I never become stingy with myself, my love, or my happiness for other people.

Homecoming

In him and through faith in him we may approach
God with freedom and confidence.

EPHESIANS 3:12

I find that when I am most in tune with Your will, it is easier for me to come to You. I can be in the middle of my workday, and a need will bring me to Your feet. When I visit a sick friend, prayers for healing and comfort form on my lips immediately.

I know people whose hearts have been broken by fathers or by authority figures in their lives. These brokenhearted folks shy away from possible hurt. Lord, Your gentle presence clears away those fears. You make room for us each time we come home to Your love. Thank You for allowing me to approach You with freedom and confidence all through the day.

Belief

The Door of Belief

*But we ought always to thank God for you,
brothers loved by the Lord, because from the
beginning God chose you to be saved through the
sanctifying work of the Spirit and through belief in
the truth.*

2 THESSALONIANS 2:13

When I walked through the door of belief and into
Your everlasting love, I understood that You chose me.
I thank You for knowing how much I would need You
all the days of my life. You saw the hurts and the difficulties I would face, and You promised to be here for
me—even before I was born.

Allow me to have a godly perspective so that
"believer" is not just a label or a way to separate myself
from others. Belief is a gift from You. It unites me with
You.

Yes, Lord

When he had gone indoors, the blind men came to him, and he asked them, "Do you believe that I am able to do this?"

"Yes, Lord," they replied.

MATTHEW 9:28

I will just say it, Lord. A desire of my heart is to have someone to love who loves me. I try not to think about it too much because I don't want to miss out on the goodness of the life I do have. I trained myself to not complain about this missing piece in my life. Along the way, I also discovered how good I feel about myself as a single person.

Today, I pray for Your leading in the area of love. I say, "Yes, Lord, I believe." I believe You are able to open my eyes to the possibility of love. Until that day comes, help me rest in the truth that my identity is not based on my marital status but on my belief in You.

Tossing and Turning

If any of you lacks wisdom, he should ask God,
who gives generously to all without finding fault,
and it will be given to him. But when he asks,
he must believe and not doubt, because he who
doubts is like a wave of the sea, blown and tossed
by the wind.

JAMES 1:5-6

I spent another sleepless night because of worries that plagued my every thought. The moment I surfaced to toss or turn, my anxieties squelched my peace. Lord, I want to have the kind of belief that releases my concerns to Your care. Right now I keep watch over my problems like I am the one in control.

Free me of this micromanagement of my life. I have faith that You will tend to my needs as the Shepherd who loves His flock. Even when I don't know how tomorrow will turn out, I have peace in You.

Do I Have That?

Jesus turned and saw her. "Take heart, daughter,"
he said, "your faith has healed you." And the
woman was healed from that moment.

MATTHEW 9:22

I think of the woman You healed, Lord. You called her daughter and said her faith healed her. Do I have that kind of faith, Lord? I know that You hear the cries of my heart and mend the broken places of my spirit. But when I reach out to touch the hem of Your garment, do I have the kind of faith that changes things?

Lord, I leave my path up to You. Each day I try to have more faith. But in the moments when it is difficult for me to reach out, please give me the belief I need. I long to hear You call me Your child.

Community

Seeing Myself

*Each of you should look not only to your own
interests, but also to the interests of others.*

PHILIPPIANS 2:4

I have gone through many phases in my single life.
There was a time I tried to do anything and everything. It was my goal to be the busiest person I knew
so nobody would think my life was empty. Then I
stopped. And I started keeping everybody out. "Why
put forth the effort? I'm alone," I thought.

But Your gentle voice reminded me to pace myself
and to live fully. Even though I live alone, I know I
don't *live* alone. Once You opened my eyes to the needs
of others, I noticed my neighbor who faced loss, the
friend who needed to talk, and for the first time, I saw
me—the person who is far from alone.

For the Greater Good

*Let us discern for ourselves what is right; let us
learn together what is good.*

JOB 34:4

Lead me to those people who are doing good, Lord.
Guide my steps and my choices so I am in the presence
of people who love You and who work as Your hands.
I stand with a solid understanding of what is right and
what is wrong, but when I stand alone, I feel unin-
spired. I need the encouragement and community of
others to step up my giving and my abundant living.

I want to be counted as one of Your faithful children. But I don't always know where to begin. Direct
me to the groups or gatherings where You need me.
Give me the confidence to join a community that seeks
Your goodness.

Part of the Body

Just as each of us has one body with many members, and these members do not all have the same function, so in Christ we who are many form one body, and each member belongs to all the others.

ROMANS 12:4-5

God, what does the body of Christ look like from afar? Is it a circle? An undistinguishable blob? A river? Are there sections trying to go their own way? I wonder about these things sometimes when I spend time with other believers. I realize how often my own priorities or purposes dictate how I interact with others or how well I follow.

Teach me to be a contributing member of the body of Christ. Allow me to recognize and appreciate my unique abilities and gifts—and then have me use them for Your purposes.

Singled Out

*If you have any encouragement from being united
with Christ, if any comfort from his love, if any
fellowship with the Spirit, if any tenderness and
compassion, then make my joy complete by being
like-minded, having the same love, being one in
spirit and purpose.*

PHILIPPIANS 2:1-2

Some of my friends are married now. Some even
have kids. I have mentally separated their lives and
concerns from my own. I love them, and I consider
their friendship gifts—but somewhere along the way,
I considered myself apart from them.

Lord, reunite my heart with theirs in the Spirit.
Remove any barriers I create. When I feel distant from
those people who are part of my life, draw me close to
someone. And when I am singled out for being single,
restore my sense of unity in Christ. Allow me to witness
the beauty and joy of wholeness and community.

Possibility

Inspired

If I rise on the wings of the dawn,
if I settle on the far side of the sea,
even there your hand will guide me,
your right hand will hold me fast.

PSALM 139:9-10

Today I faced a very new situation. The entire time I was praying for Your help and guidance. I knew I wouldn't find the right words on my own. When I am nervous, I lose all sense of direction. This time I was smart enough to look in Your direction, and You were there.

Your right hand holds me fast so I can step into what life offers. You give me the words when I need them. You push me forward when I am tempted to hold back. Lord, You are my foundation. Next time I face a possibility, an opportunity, or a dream, I know right where to look for inspiration.

The Perfect Formula

Give, and it will be given to you. A good measure,
pressed down, shaken together and running over,
will be poured into your lap. For with the measure
you use, it will be measured to you.

LUKE 6:38

Lord, in Your perfect way there is a formula for a full life. We have to give to receive. I need to give my life over to You in order to receive the wonders You have for me. When I am tempted to hold tightly to my blessings or my ideas or even myself, open up my heart.

May I always see the chance to give as a limitless opportunity to express Your compassion, acceptance, and eternal love. Following the formula You have set in motion, I will measure a day's goodness by the greatness of my giving.

Do Gooders

*Therefore, as we have opportunity, let us do good
to all people, especially to those who belong to the
family of believers.*

GALATIANS 6:10

My patience is running thin. I don't always handle
it well when people feel bad for me because I am single.
It is equally difficult to be gracious when they rattle off
the short list of other eligible people they know—and
it is the same short list the last person had.

But God, I am beginning to understand that it is
my pride interfering with the good efforts of others.
People do mean well. And these are Christian friends
and family. Let me receive their kindness with a deeper
sense of connection to the family of believers. And who
knows, maybe there is a possibility on that short list
after all.

What Is...

Jesus replied, "What is impossible with men is possible with God."

LUKE 18:27

When I cannot dream, You dream for me. When I cannot rise to the challenge, You do it for me. When I wonder if I am worth it, You tell me I am. When I doubt my purpose, You present it to me with hope.

Thank You, God, for being my sole source of power, might, strength, and courage. You are the possibility to my impossibility.

Solitude

Luxury of Time

Very early in the morning, while it was still dark,
Jesus got up, left the house and went off to a
solitary place, where he prayed.

MARK 1:35

God, show me the blessings! My life is filled with incredible blessings, but often I am too bothered by some small thing to notice them. My married friends complain that they rarely get a moment to themselves. My co-workers, who put in overtime, long for a vacation. Parents feel pulled in twenty directions, no matter how many kids they have.

Reveal to me the wonders of time spent in solitude. Present me with the peace of spirit to enjoy what I have. Allow my thoughts to wind down and my body to relax. I want to spend time with You without distraction. I want to spend time with myself and grow to respect and savor the luxury of time alone.

Alone, Not Lonely

God sets the lonely in families, he leads forth the prisoners with singing; but the rebellious live in a sun-scorched land.

PSALM 68:6

Thank You, God, for placing me in a family of friends, relatives, co-workers, and neighbors. I need only to look around me to see that family can be and mean so many different things. When I needed help with a project, I knew who to call. The day I wanted someone to pray for me, a friend stopped by.

Lord, help me find comfort in You and in those You place in my life. You have set me among those willing to reach out. Move me from loneliness to belonging.

You Alone

My soul finds rest in God alone;
my salvation comes from him.
He alone is my rock and my salvation;
he is my fortress, I will never be shaken.

PSALM 62:1-2

You are my rock, my salvation, my strength, and my vision of all that is good and just. Never will this life I build be shaken and destroyed because You are the one who sees me through every battle, every storm, and every harm.

The foundation of faith I build my hopes upon will not be wiped out from beneath me. My trust is in Your remarkable power, and not in my own strength. During my times of weakness or sorrow, or when night seems never ending, I call out to You alone, for only You can save me.

When Others Leave

You will leave me all alone. Yet I am not alone, for my Father is with me.

JOHN 16:32

Lord, I might feel alone, but I know Your eyes watch over me in my times of solitude and yearning. You guide my steps carefully and with the hands of a loving Father. There is only rest when a person comes to You. In the stillness of a new day, I find my peace here in Your tender mercy.

I have had people come and go in my life. Some have disappointed me so much that I still carry the hurt along my journey. Release me from these concerns. My heart sings with the song of truth, and it resounds with the sweetness and sureness of Your presence.

Forever

Here I Stand

*But the plans of the LORD stand firm forever,
the purposes of his heart through all generations.*

PSALM 33:11

Before I was born, You knew what my forever looked like. You planted seeds of purpose in my heart. Over time You nurtured those seeds and encouraged me to grow. The legacy of Your faithfulness continues in my life.

I stand here today excited about what my future might bring. Each day that I draw closer to You, I better understand how Your plans manifest in both simple and extraordinary ways. I am thankful that as Your heir, my birthright is a future of faith.

On Schedule

*Therefore do not worry about tomorrow, for
tomorrow will worry about itself.*

MATTHEW 6:34

It seems like I am always comparing my life plan
to that of others. I wonder if I am behind schedule for
all that I hope to have or accomplish. God, forgive me
for this constant and worthless use of energy. Grant me
the discipline to break the habit of letting my concerns
for tomorrow control my today.

My life will unfold in the way You intended for me.
There is comfort in knowing I do not need to catch up
with anyone else's plan. I have a custom-made life, and
I am right on schedule.

Excited

"For I know the plans I have for you," declares the
LORD, "plans to prosper you and not to harm you,
plans to give you hope and a future."

JEREMIAH 29:11

Amazing! Right now I am participating in the plan
You have for me. I didn't just wake up to any ordinary
day—I took another step toward the future You have
for me. When I flip through my mental photo album
of memories, I can see how You have protected me and
led me through the peaks and valleys of my journey.

Through the power of faith, I have a purpose and
my life has meaning. My hope extends beyond my
today and into the future because You have made it
so. I'm excited to see what You have in store.

Wisdom

*God understands the way to it
and he alone knows where it dwells,
for he views the ends of the earth
and sees everything under the heavens.*

JOB 28:23-24

Wisdom and understanding escape most of us. We look for it in all the wrong places. But You, Lord, know the way to it. Your eyes can see the place where it dwells and where it flows through time and through creation. I pray for Your wisdom. I want to carry it within me for the rest of my life.

I don't know what forever will bring, but if I live in Your wisdom and Your way, I trust the journey. It is in Your hands, and they formed the world. How simple for You to shape my future.

Perception

Where's My Worth?

*How can you believe if you accept praise from one
another, yet make no effort to obtain the praise
that comes from the only God?*

JOHN 5:44

My sense of self-worth rises too seldom and falls
too easily. Even constructive criticism from a friend or
even a stranger can cause me to question my abilities. I
can easily pick out what I don't like about my body or
my looks. This is not how or who I want to be, Lord.
And it is a disservice to all the blessings and strengths
in my life.

Grant me a shift in perspective. When my thoughts
are skewed and my sense of value is distorted by the
world's view of perfection, show me how to receive
the most important love of all—Yours. Give me eyes
to see my worth through Your eyes and call it good,
perfect, and whole.

In the Light

*He gives wisdom to the wise
and knowledge to the discerning.
He reveals deep and hidden things;
he knows what lies in darkness,
and light dwells with him.*

DANIEL 2:21-22

When there is darkness, You shed light. Where there is uncertainty, You remove the shadows. Where there is brokenness, You offer healing. Where deception is buried, You resurrect truth.

God, in every situation the brightness of Your wisdom brings goodness and righteousness to light. Your Word is my source of knowledge and direction. Your never-changing precepts shape my perception of all that I experience.

A Process

You were taught, with regard to your former way of life, to put off your old self, which is being corrupted by its deceitful desires; to be made new in the attitude of your minds; and to put on the new self, created to be like God in true righteousness and holiness.

EPHESIANS 4:22-24

There is a process in place for change. God, You give me a path to newness in mind and spirit. You not only offer refreshment, but transformation as well. I can try something new—a hobby, a sport, a job—and even if the change is successful, it is temporary. But, Lord, Your changes start from within and manifest in my life in different ways. They are there to stay, and they are intended to be with me forever.

I like how my mind works. There is great pleasure in learning, knowing, and growing in understanding. You allow for this deepening of my awareness and, in return, my life is changed and my thoughts shift from temporal to eternal.

Making a Way

See, I am doing a new thing!
Now it springs up; do you not perceive it?
I am making a way in the desert
and streams in the wasteland.

ISAIAH 43:19

It is all I want, Lord—to make my way through this life with a sense of purpose and a perspective that reflects Your heart for others. Because I am responsible for my earthly needs, I turn to You as my provider and my strength. There was a time when this caused me to be self-focused. I was forgetting that my life was intended for so much more.

My heart's desire is not to make *my* way through life, but to find *Your* way to everlasting life. Carve out a path for the streams of the living water in the desert of my need. Deliver me from my selfishness so that I might discover the new things You have for me.

Trust

Lighting the Way

*Your word is a lamp to my feet and a light for
my path.*

PSALM 119:105

I always take a flashlight with me when I am
camping because there are so few light sources and it's
so dark. I'm beginning to see how Your Word is my
source of light and wisdom to get through my days.
It reveals the pitfalls and the peaks, and it guides my
every step.

The world has so few light sources. Thank You,
Lord, for being my lamp, my sun, my inner light, and
the light unto the world.

As Sure as the Sun

Let us acknowledge the LORD; let us press on to
acknowledge him. As surely as the sun rises,
he will appear; he will come to us like the winter
rains, like the spring rains that water the earth.

HOSEA 6:3

I awaken each day with the certainty that I will be
greeted by the dawn. I welcome the joys and the challenges ahead. And with each day, You offer the certainty
of fellowship and renewal—I just need to acknowledge
and trust Your truths.

Shower me with blessings, circumstances for
growth, and opportunities to know You better. You
come like the rains and the sunshine into my life to
refresh and nourish me. I praise You.

Should I?

*Commit to the LORD whatever you do, and your
plans will succeed.*

PROVERBS 16:3

Should I, Lord? I've been thinking about a certain
decision lately, but it would involve trusting You completely. You know how reserved I have been about such
things—is this the time for me to take the plunge? I
try to do so much on my own. I have even prided
myself on this acquired skill. But when I have success,
is it really what You wanted for me? And if I fail, is it
because I have not listened to You?

Commitment is a scary word and an even scarier
action. Help me trust You, Lord. Where there is doubt,
fill me with Your confidence. I want to succeed in
faith.

Dwelling Place

*Trust in the LORD and do good; dwell in the land
and enjoy safe pasture. Delight yourself in the
LORD and he will give you the desires of your
heart.*

PSALM 37:3-4

I might move five times in my life, or more...but
my home is always with You, Lord. Over the years You
have shown me time after time how faithful You are to
those who trust You. My insecurities lead me astray, but
my faith always returns me to Your presence.

My delight is in You and Your goodness. Teach me
to trust Your purposes for my life and shape the desires
of my heart to fulfill Your perfect will.

Expectations

The Promise of Waiting

In the morning, O LORD, you hear my voice; in the morning I lay my requests before you and wait in expectation.

PSALM 5:3

I never viewed waiting as a pleasant experience, Lord. I expected what I wanted, when I wanted it. But You have shown me Your care during the waiting hours. I have heard Your voice in the whisper of morning and the tiptoe silence of night.

Today I place my need for direction and instruction at Your feet and I wait. You provide all that I need during this time of anticipation. Now I understand that the promise of waiting is hope.

Chasing the Next Big Thing

*So do not worry, saying, "What shall we eat?" or
"What shall we drink?" or "What shall we wear?"
For the pagans run after all these things, and your
heavenly Father knows that you need them. But
seek first his kingdom and his righteousness, and
all these things will be given to you as well.*

MATTHEW 6:31-33

In a culture of trends and fads, I lose sight of the
differences between what I want and what I need. Have
I come to expect anything and everything from Your
hand, Lord? My worries about "having it all" fill my
prayers. Turn my heart toward a desire for righteousness and faith.

You care for my basic needs. I need not fret over
the material things that flow in and out of my hands. I
need not be consumed with expectations of wealth and
fame. As a child of the King, I have the freedom to let
go of such things and embrace the hope of Your care.

Misleading

Do not conform any longer to the pattern of this world, but be transformed by the renewing of your mind. Then you will be able to test and approve what God's will is—his good, pleasing and perfect will.

ROMANS 12:2

The patterns of the world are misleading. They promise a kaleidoscope of wonder and endless opportunities. But I find it difficult to concentrate on any of these glittery delights. Through my lens of faith, I can focus on the prize of eternal life. My eyes can take in every bit of the colorful promise of the rainbow. And my heart can rest in Your will.

When I place my hope and my dreams in the palm of Your hand, the confusing distractions of the world fade away, and my eyes remain fixed on Your will.

What Is the Right Choice?

I sought the LORD, and he answered me; he delivered me from all my fears.

PSALM 34:4

God, I am at a crossroad. I don't know which way to go. Friends have advice; I have my inclinations. But I am fearful. My feet don't want to budge. I have made mistakes and miscalculations before. My spirit has been crushed by broken expectations.

Lord, I am coming to You today completely in awe of Your mercy and Your faithfulness. I seek Your wisdom. I want Your confidence as I step forward. Please deliver me from doubt so I can discover the fullness of life.

Purpose

Your Power

It does not, therefore, depend on man's desire or effort, but on God's mercy. For the Scripture says to Pharaoh: "I raised you up for this very purpose, that I might display my power in you and that my name might be proclaimed in all the earth."

ROMANS 9:16-17

Some people don't see the full me. They know I am single; they know I am a person of faith. They see the job I have and the friends I have made. But Lord, when I take risks, when I make leaps of faith, may they truly see You and Your power.

Only You can lift me up to a place of influence or strength. May I tell everyone what You have done in my life. May Your great purposes be seen in the smallest actions of my day.

My Work, My Purpose

The man who plants and the man who waters
have one purpose, and each will be rewarded
according to his own labor. For we are God's fellow
workers; you are God's field, God's building.

1 CORINTHIANS 3:8-9

I'm not raising a family. I'm not supporting a spouse.
But the labor You have given me is just as important,
vital, and significant to the building of Your purpose.
Why do I forget this? I take from Your plan by regret-
ting or coveting the labor of others.

Lord, I want to praise You with all that I do. May
I find pleasure and a measure for contentment and
ministry in the work You give me each day.

Beneath It All

*Many are the plans in a man's heart, but it is the
LORD's purpose that prevails.*

PROVERBS 19:21

Beneath my actions and my dreams, my hopes and
my efforts is a current of purpose set in motion by
Your hand. As much as I seek Your heart, I am not
always certain if my desires are of Your great plan for
me. But day by day I give to You my devotion and my
best intentions.

Please mold my human efforts into Your divine
plan. Create in me a sensitivity to Your leading so that
I serve a purpose bigger than my own.

Encouraged

My purpose is that they may be encouraged in heart and united in love, so that they may have the full riches of complete understanding, in order that they may know the mystery of God, namely, Christ, in whom are hidden all the treasures of wisdom and knowledge.

COLOSSIANS 2:2-3

When I am discouraged, I take heart in the love You show me. I have witnessed Your mercy in the kindness of others, Your peace in the blessing of friendship, Your wisdom in the Word. These glimpses of who You are add dimension and clarity to my understanding of what gives this life meaning. You are my purpose. And Your love lifts me out of my moments of despair and fills my heart with treasures of eternity.

Relationship

Honest

*Therefore each of you must put off falsehood and
speak truthfully to his neighbor, for we are all
members of one body.*

EPHESIANS 4:25

I'm not always good at being sociable. I want to be
involved in the lives of other people, but, God, sometimes it is difficult to be myself around others. Making
new friends is not easy, even when they are Christians.
I find that my old insecurities rise up and take over my
personality when I step into a room of strangers.

Lord, give me the confidence and courage I need to
speak from the heart with others and show them the
real me. You created me, and I should take comfort in
this life I lead and the person I have grown to be. As
I speak to others, give me a heart for their concerns,
needs, and insecurities so we can all be open with one
another.

Single Service

*Each one should use whatever gift he has received
to serve others, faithfully administering God's
grace in its various forms.*

1 PETER 4:10

Stepping out to serve You is not always easy as a single person. I prefer the buddy system, and often You provide just the right person to join me for certain tasks or commitments. But there are also tugs at my heart that are for me alone. I sense You are leading me toward a particular way of serving You, but I am scared to go it alone.

Allow me to let go of my personal worries and lack of confidence so that I can embrace Your strength and purpose. Maybe my presence will help others become involved. Maybe I will discover something about myself by following through with this impulse. No matter what, I know I will learn what faithfulness looks like.

Something Good

I pray that you may be active in sharing your faith, so that you will have a full understanding of every good thing we have in Christ.

PHILEMON 1:6

Because of my faith in You, I have something worth sharing. Help me pass along the perfect promises of faith to others even though I am fallible and imperfect. I may not always think of the right words, but I have faith in Your Word. I might stumble or falter, but then Your power of grace will be noticed.

When I trust You and express the goodness of Christ to people in my life, I become more in tune with Your love for them. My heart opens up to include people and to accept them—just as Your heart does every day.

Love

Beyond Self

*May the Lord direct your hearts into God's love
and Christ's perseverance.*

2 THESSALONIANS 3:5

Beyond me there is knowledge of You. When I get past my hang-ups, my selfish thoughts, and my personal pain, there is a sea of love that flows under Your command. When I look past my issues, my prejudices, and my judgments, there is a horizon of promises and hope.

Lord, I am beginning to see how I can go beyond myself. Keep me from staying caught up in my own life so much that I miss the chance to experience and share Your unconditional love.

Always

*Love is patient, love is kind. It does not envy, it
does not boast, it is not proud. It is not rude, it is
not self-seeking, it is not easily angered, it keeps no
record of wrongs. Love does not delight in evil but
rejoices with the truth. It always protects, always
trusts, always hopes, always perseveres.*

1 CORINTHIANS 13:4-7

I hear the "Love is" verses every time I go to a wedding. It moves me each time. My heart can get caught up in what it doesn't have right now, but underneath that ache is peace. I have experienced the purest love straight from the Creator of love Himself. You have shown me selfless, truthful, and sweet love.

In my life, I have directly seen Your hand of protection and guidance. Never in my moments of loss or pain have I felt alone. And best of all, I do believe that love is that gift in my heart that allows me to always hope.

The Strength of Love

*Be on your guard; stand firm in the faith; be men
of courage; be strong. Do everything in love.*

1 CORINTHIANS 16:13-14

It isn't easy to love. There are some people who
seem difficult to embrace with warmth and kindness.
I lose sight of how to love when I am around them. I
have even caught myself being a bit indifferent toward
those I know You call me to love.

Expand my view of what love is. Stretch the limited
walls of my human heart to make room for everybody I
am meant to care for. Direct my actions so I act coura-
geously on behalf of those in need. Allow me to stand
firmly on the foundation of love.

Love for All

The LORD is righteous in all his ways
and loving toward all he has made.
The LORD is near to all who call on him,
to all who call on him in truth.

PSALM 145:17-18

Why am I so careful about who I love? When I face the chance to make a new friend, I am thankful...but I am also hesitant. I'm afraid of what that commitment might mean. If I meet a stranger in need, I hold back my smile and my willingness to extend grace. Fear keeps me from loving as You love.

You are near to me and to those who call out Your name in moments of praise and despair. May I sincerely reach out to those You have made. May I love with Your love.

Acceptance

Still

*O LORD, you have searched me
and you know me.
You know when I sit and when I rise;
you perceive my thoughts from afar.*

PSALM 139:1-2

You know me inside and out, and You *still* love me. You have searched my depths and counted my tears and eased my worries. Nothing I do goes unnoticed by my God. The sins I have brought to Your feet have been swept away by the rain of Your mercy. My failures, complaints, and rants have been forgotten.

There are no obstacles between me and Your acceptance. You have had to clear away all my excuses and barriers. And You still love me.

Known

*Keep on loving each other as brothers. Do not
forget to entertain strangers, for by so doing some
people have entertained angels without knowing it.*

HEBREWS 13:1-2

I had some great conversations with strangers re-
cently. Normally I am too shy or intimidated or busy
to share in conversation with people I do not know.
But when there is something in common that sparks
a connection with another person, it leads to a real
connection.

It is silly how many times I have not followed my
impulse to reach out to someone else because of my
fear of rejection. Carry me through this initial doubt.
And remind me that even when I don't know the
person, the person is known and loved by You.

Can You Hear Me?

You are forgiving and good, O Lord, abounding in love to all who call to you.

PSALM 86:5

Lord, hear my prayers today. I have much to bring to You. My mind and heart are filled with concerns and praises. As soon as I opened my eyes this morning, I was aware of how much I needed to talk to You. I kept my distance for a while because of feelings of shame. My stubbornness caused me to feel unloved and unwanted.

But You are my Redeemer and my Savior. I need not return to my old patterns of thinking and behavior. I can come to You anytime because You love me, You forgive me, and You accept me. I have so much to tell You.

Letting Go

Remember not the sins of my youth
and my rebellious ways;
according to your love remember me,
for you are good, O LORD.

PSALM 25:7

How many times have You called me to let go of my concerns and accept my own circumstances? How many times have You whispered "Let go" regarding my past sins? For a long time I kept thinking You must have a bad memory when it came to my mistakes. But now I understand that You saved me from them long ago. And You accept me just as I am today.

Thank You, Lord, for releasing my rebellious ways and for never letting go of me.

Passion

Inspiration

*Whatever you do, work at it with all your heart,
as working for the Lord, not for men, since you
know that you will receive an inheritance from
the Lord as a reward. It is the Lord Christ you are
serving.*

COLOSSIANS 3:23-24

I want to give You my all, Lord. Fill me with the
energy and hope I need to live this life fully. When days
seem meaningless or my efforts useless, revive me with
a sense of purpose and passion.

May I see each day as a new opportunity to show
You my love and my commitment. Free me from regret
so that I can accept the inheritance of abundant life.
You are my inspiration and my source of motivation to
follow through with the plans You place on my heart.

Every Part of Me

*Jesus replied: "Love the Lord your God with
all your heart and with all your soul and with
all your mind." This is the first and greatest
commandment.*

MATTHEW 22:37-38

I can count on my fingers the times I have given
100 percent. How sad is that? I want to be the person
who gives more than that to You on a regular basis.
Help me discover what the passionate and compassionate life can lead to.

Give me a heart for Your heart. Better yet, I will give
You my heart, my soul, and my mind so that I am fully
Yours. Jesus' call to follow the greatest commandment
will be what carries me through the days when I am
tempted to settle for less.

Out My Window

They will speak of the glorious splendor of your majesty, and I will meditate on your wonderful works. They will tell of the power of your awesome works, and I will proclaim your great deeds.

PSALM 145:5-6

The splendor of Your majesty and might can be seen out my window. Your glorious creation sways in the breeze and follows the seasons guided by Your plan. Every part of nature speaks of Your wonder. When I am feeling insignificant, I glance beyond the curtains and realize I am part of Your awesome works. You included me in Your plan for this world.

Give me the spark of passion I need to proclaim Your great deeds. May I become like the majestic trees, sure and brilliant, so that my life might speak of Your love even when words cannot be found.

Taking My Cues

*This is how we know that we love the children
of God: by loving God and carrying out his
commands. This is love for God: to obey his
commands.*

1 JOHN 5:2-3

Passion is considered many things in today's culture. As a believer, I understand passion to be a combi-
nation of commitment and effort to follow Your heart.
Ignite the desire in me to serve others and to seek out
the best for those in my life. Create in me a heart that
is on fire with Your love and compassion for others.

I know I will still question You sometimes because
I will be afraid of the risk involved in loving Your children. But I believe a bigger and better life awaits the
person who obeys and cherishes Your commands.

Purity

Life Preserver

How I long for your precepts! Preserve my life in your righteousness.

PSALM 119:40

Throw me a rope, a line, a flotation device—I am sinking! I was trying to do something on my own again, and now I am in need of help. I've made a mess of things and have nobody to blame except my stubborn self. Well, Lord, I am catching on to this pattern in my life. So today I am asking for help.

I long for Your precepts, Your guidance, and Your assistance. When I hold on to Your gifts of preservation and survival, I lead a righteous life. You clean up the mess and make me pure. And all I need to do is hold on to Your lifesaving Word.

Peace Offering

The fruit of righteousness will be peace; the effect of righteousness will be quietness and confidence forever.

ISAIAH 32:17

Lord, the blessing of a righteous life is peace. How I crave to have peace in my days! You know me. I tend to worry or turn situations into complications. But when my thoughts are purely about You and Your will, my heart is calmed, my soul soothed.

Still my spirit today. Breathe new confidence into my mind and walk me toward the future with confidence. You renew me in righteousness and lead me to a place of peace and effectiveness.

Pure and Simple

"Martha, Martha," the Lord answered, "you are worried and upset about many things, but only one thing is needed. Mary has chosen what is better, and it will not be taken away from her."

LUKE 10:41-42

I sure do make life complicated, don't I? You don't need to answer that, Lord. I hear my own thoughts and watch my actions with dismay. I am quick to blame others when things go wrong. My truth is based on me and not on You. I get so caught up in the acts of fretting and fussing that I lose sight of that one thing I need—time with You.

Lord, I want a pure and simple relationship with You. I want to put aside the many distractions and sit at Your feet, ready and willing to know You better.

Security

Eyes on You

*If I have put my trust in gold or said to pure gold,
"You are my security," if I have rejoiced over my
great wealth, the fortune my hands had gained,
if I have regarded the sun in its radiance or the
moon moving in splendor, so that my heart was
secretly enticed and my hand offered them a kiss
of homage, then these also would be sins to be
judged, for I would have been unfaithful to God
on high.*

JOB 31:24-28

Like a magician telling me to watch the coin beneath
the swirling, twirling cups...my eyes try to follow the
money in my life. Where will the wealth be for me?
How will I provide for my future? When I am really sad
about my situation, I start examining how hard my life
is because I have only myself to depend on.

This is when You stop my crazy thinking. I turn my
eyes back to my only source of security and life—You.
Your face radiates with the brightness of my future, and
I know I don't need to look any further.

Rich in Spirit

However, there should be no poor among you, for in the land the LORD your God is giving you to possess as your inheritance, he will richly bless you, if only you fully obey the LORD your God and are careful to follow all these commands I am giving you today.

DEUTERONOMY 15:4-5

I am learning to rest in the riches of my faith. Your children are never poor in spirit, and I am so thankful. My desires for the things of the world lessen as my hope in the matters of eternity increase.

There is a fullness in my heart when I think of the day I came to You, asking for Your love. To this day, that love overflows into and through every part of my life. I am grateful for my inheritance. It gives me a richer today and a brighter tomorrow.

Single Hour

Who of you by worrying can add a single hour to his life? Since you cannot do this very little thing, why do you worry about the rest?

LUKE 12:25-26

I have spent many hours alone. The single life affords me the luxury of solitude, but it also causes me to spend many moments worrying about my life. It isn't that I'm not happy with my life—I feel blessed in many ways. But when I have the television on for company or I seek out distractions to avoid sensing I'm alone, then I have not yet turned over my life to Your care.

Who am I to think I can change anything by fretting about yesterday or today? Teach me to relax. I do not want to spend one more hour serving the god of worry when the God of life and hope is my Lord.

Because

You will be secure, because there is hope; you will look about you and take your rest in safety.

JOB 11:18

My life has drifted. There have been times when I have felt confused about my faith and my personal path. What are You doing, Lord? What would You have *me* do? I have struggled with the meaning of life. It is a cliché, but it is also the truth.

But You call me to look around. You ask me to take inventory of my life and see the proof of Your love and direction. Here I finally find peace. I can make sense of my days because there is hope in all You have done for me.

Hope

With Your Hand

*You open your hand and satisfy the desires of every
living thing.*

PSALM 145:16

With Your hand You shape the sky and earth. You
plan the days of many and orchestrate how the lives
intersect and create community. Everything big and
small is managed by You. I don't always come to You
with my desires. I feel selfish or self-centered to say
that I want the love of others.

Yet when my heart has been broken, it is Your hand
that molds the pieces back into the shape of hope. I
believe in the goodness that comes from Your hands.

Said It Before

Find rest, O my soul, in God alone; my hope comes from him.

PSALM 62:5

If I have told myself once, I have told myself a million times: It is You alone who gives me hope. People fail me. My lofty goals fail me. Even my hard work can let me down. Lord, my soul and my spirit were born of Your grace, and they will only find hope within Your embrace.

I wonder what my later years will be like. Will I find happiness? Sorrow? Peace? All of these? Today, with faith, I understand that it will not matter what the future brings. My soul will find rest and hope in Your limitless love.

As the Day Is Long

Show me your ways, O LORD, teach me your
paths; guide me in your truth and teach me,
for you are God my Savior, and my hope is in you
all day long.

PSALM 25:4-5

My love for You is as deep as the day is long. My hand reaches as far as it can to touch Your face. My feet step forth with the desire to follow Your paths. Lord, You guide me and gently navigate my steps. When I am lost, You bring me back into the safety of Your pasture.

My hope is in You all day long because You care for me. When I wasn't a person of faith, You still protected me and brought me into this place of strength and possibility. Lord, I pray for my hope to multiply so that I might bring a Christlike attitude into my life in every way.

I'm Waiting

I wait for the Lord, my soul waits, and in his word
I put my hope.

PSALM 130:5

∽

It isn't easy. I had a plan for how my life would look and feel by this age. Those things have not happened, and I find myself waiting patiently. Okay, not so patiently. The clock of "want" ticks with every passing day. Every part of me longs for the achievement and success I had planned.

God, take from me the desires that are not of You. Place my hope in the eternal wonder of Your perfect plan. Waiting is only wasting time if it does not lead me to You.

Now I Know

I know what it is to be in need, and I know what it is to have plenty. I have learned the secret of being content in any and every situation, whether well fed or hungry, whether living in plenty or in want. I can do everything through him who gives me strength.

PHILIPPIANS 4:12-13

I rush about taking care of the details each day's work requires. Sure, I am taking responsibility and managing my life. But now I know that no matter how old I get, there is no such thing as a life independent of You, Lord. At least that would not be a life I would want.

My past efforts to clear my days of trouble or my heart of pain or my future of strife carry me through a cycle of highs and lows. I thought I knew the secrets to living a strong, independent, single life. Now I know—I am utterly, wholly, and forever dependent upon You.

The One-Minute Prayers™ Series

HARVEST HOUSE
PUBLISHERS

Books You Can Believe In*
HARVEST HOUSE PUBLISHERS

Discovering Your Divine Assignment
Robin Chaddock

God loves you and has a purpose for your life—a "divine assignment" that will fulfill your deepest longings. Informative, easy-to-read chapters include fun and challenging questions to help you explore your beliefs, your passions, and your goals as you uncover your primary passion and greatest strength.

Overcoming the 7 Obstacles to Spiritual Growth
Dwight Carlson

Have you taken a detour in your spiritual journey? Dwight explores the obstacles that hinder faith and reveals the steps you can take to overcome them and grow in the Lord. You can look forward to an extraordinary life as you embrace the challenges and triumphs of living in Christ!

Small Changes for a Better Life
Elizabeth George

Don't settle for okay when best is in sight! Are you almost happy? Is success just out of reach? Whether your life needs minor adjustments or a major overhaul, Elizabeth helps you pinpoint problems and then reveals small changes you can make to transform your life and excel in all areas of your life.

The Prayer That Changes Everything®
Stormie Omartian

Prayer is powerful! Packed with personal stories, biblical truths, and practical principles about offering praise in the middle of difficulties, sorrow, fear, and yes, abundance and joy, *The Prayer That Changes Everything* encourages you to "live each day making praise your reaction and not a last resort."

7 Simple Steps to a Healthier You
Dawn Hall

Dawn offers inspiration and surefire steps to help you embrace a healthy lifestyle. On this journey to physical, emotional, and spiritual fitness, you'll discover advice for handling weight issues, hectic schedules, and unhealthy behaviors. You'll also find exercise and food plans that will work best for you.

Conversations with Jesus
Calvin Miller

A celebrated poet and preacher, Calvin offers a creative, intimate way to listen to Christ. Daily devotions include a Bible verse, a prayer, and Jesus' response in first-person narrative. This fresh look at Jesus reveals His love for God, humankind, and His followers. Experience a faith that is richer and deeper!